Full Throttle

Ford Thunderbird

Tracy Nelson Maurer

Rourke
Publishing LLC
Vero Beach, Florida 32964

D1716673

www.rourkepublishing.com

PHOTO CREDITS: Page 7: Courtesy of the United States Air Force; All other photos: Courtesy of Ford Motor Company

Project Assistance: Lou Paliani, President, Vintage Thunderbird Club International

Also, the author extends appreciation to Julie Lundgren, Timothy Vacula, Mike Maurer, Lois M. Nelson, and the team at Rourke Publishing.

Editor: Robert Stengard-Olliges
Page Design: Tara Raymo

Library of Congress Cataloging-in-Publication Data

Maurer, Tracy, 1965-
  Ford Thunderbird / Tracy Nelson Maurer.
      p. cm. -- (Full throttle 2)
  Includes bibliographical references and index.
  ISBN 978-1-60044-572-9
  1. Thunderbird automobile--Juvenile literature. I. Title.
  TL215.T46M37 2008
  629.222'2--dc22
                                    2007014845

Printed in the USA

1G/1G

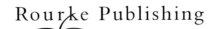

Rourke Publishing

www.rourkepublishing.com – rourke@rourkepublishing.com
Post Office Box 3328, Vero Beach, FL 32964

Table of Contents

The Classy Chassis

For more than fifty years, the Ford Thunderbird has dazzled American car buyers with its trendy styling and posh interiors. It first appeared at the 1954 Detroit Auto Show. Ford expected about 10,000 orders for the sleek 1955 model. It sold more than 16,000. The two-seater purred with "personal luxury" to attract buyers away from the recently introduced Chevrolet Corvette.

The sporty Thunderbird could fly on a straight stretch, but it lacked the **acceleration** and handling of a true sports car. No matter. Its playful look and cushy comfort made the car an instant classic.

To gain speed for the car, Ford's designers lightened it. They chopped more than one foot off its length compared to other 1950s Fords. The "classy *chassis*" still weighed well over 3,000 pounds.

Fast Fact

In October 1954, Ford received more than 3,500 orders in just 10 days for the new 1955 T-Bird.

acceleration
    an increase in speed
chassis
    the frame that supports
    the body of a vehicle

Fast Fact

The hood scoop hid the bulge from the motor's air cleaner.

Ford set the 1955 Thunderbird's base price below $3,000—hundreds less than a Corvette's. Thunderbirds stole Chevrolet's thunder. Corvette sales dipped from over 3,000 cars in 1954 to 700 in 1955.

5

A Legendary Name

Many Native American legends described a powerful Thunderbird that used its huge wings to conjure wind, thunder, lightning, and rain. The creature's name sounded bold and free-spirited. A Ford employee entered it in the company's naming contest for the new two-seater. His prize? A dandy new suit!

Fast Fact

Between 1955 to 1957, all Thunderbirds came with removable hardtops. A fabric convertible top was an option. Today, collectors prize the rarer fabric convertibles.

Before Ford named its legendary car, the U.S. Air Force adopted the "Thunderbird" name in 1953 for its amazing 3600th Air Demonstration Team. The Thunderbirds still fly in air shows today.

Ford started tweaking the Thunderbird almost immediately. The 1956 model featured snazzy windows in the hardtop. The portholes improved the driver's rear view and added unforgettable flair.

Fast Fact

The 1957 Thunderbird featured a radio that shifted its volume to match the engine speed. More vvvvroom = louder tunes.

Thunderbirds could cruise America's highways at 100 mph (160 km/h)—legally in a few places. Each state set its own speed limits back then. Montana and Nevada had no posted rural limits. The energy crisis pushed the U.S. government to set a national speed limit of 55 mph (88 km/h) in 1974. In 1995, the speed decision went back to the states.

Ford added extra safety features for its 1957 Thunderbird. The car sported the first fully padded dash. It also had a safety shaped steering wheel, safety door latches, and a shatter resistant mirror. Seat belts were optional.

President Eisenhower signed the law to start the Interstate Highway Program in 1956. Building the system took more than ten years.

The National Highway Traffic Safety Administration issued its first safety belt rules in 1967.

Always Changing

While Corvette stayed true to its two seater sports car heritage over the years, Thunderbird soared on the winds of change to earn its place in automobile history. Ford made major updates to the Thunderbird design almost every three years. The company tried more than forty tweaks along the way to satisfy American trends.

THUNDERBIRD MILESTONES

Years	Nickname	Style File
1955-1957	Little Birds	Two seaters with porthole hardtops
1958-1960	Square Birds	Four seaters with hints of tail fins
1961-1963	Bullet Birds	Bullet shape; optional rear seat cover for deuce look
1964-1966	Sculpted Birds	Last T-Bird convertible until 2002
1967-1969	Big Birds	Hideaway headlights; no rear fender skirts
1970-1972	Bigger Birds	Beak grille; whale-sized at 216"
1973-1976	Biggest Birds	Luxury liner sized up to 225.6" long and 79.3" wide
1977-1979	Diet Birds	Dropped 1,000 pounds and six times faster
1980-1982	Box Birds	Shrank again to about 200" long
1983-1997	Aero Birds	Sleek lines, turbocharged engines for real speed
2002-2005	Retro Birds	Fifties flashback with kicky two seater style

Will the Thunderbird rise again like a phoenix or is it done like a turkey?

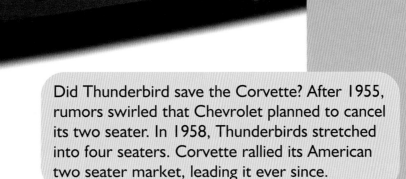

concept car
a vehicle built to try out new looks and techniques

Did Thunderbird save the Corvette? After 1955, rumors swirled that Chevrolet planned to cancel its two seater. In 1958, Thunderbirds stretched into four seaters. Corvette rallied its American two seater market, leading it ever since.

Ford built a new assembly plant in Wixom, Michigan for the 1958 Thunderbird—and the T-Birds that followed. The plant closed in 2006.

Thunderbirds rolled out of the factory every year between 1955 and 1997, one of the longest runs for a model name.

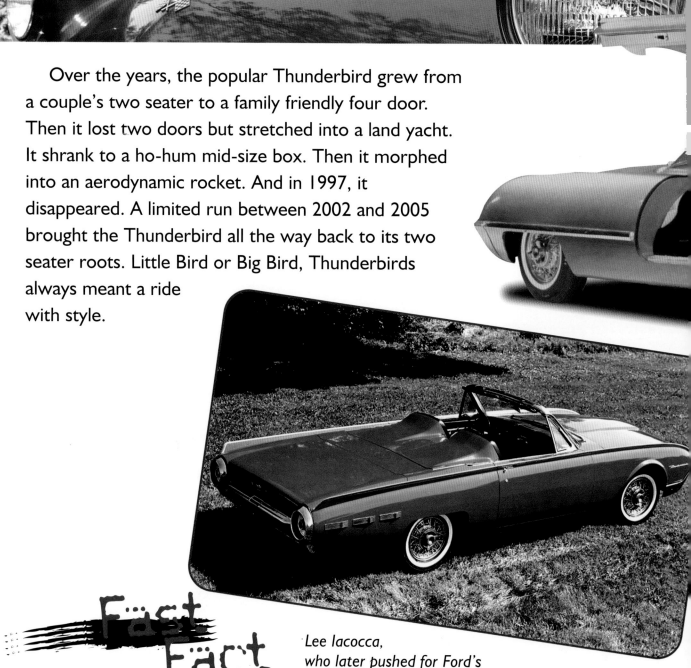

Over the years, the popular Thunderbird grew from a couple's two seater to a family friendly four door. Then it lost two doors but stretched into a land yacht. It shrank to a ho-hum mid-size box. Then it morphed into an aerodynamic rocket. And in 1997, it disappeared. A limited run between 2002 and 2005 brought the Thunderbird all the way back to its two seater roots. Little Bird or Big Bird, Thunderbirds always meant a ride with style.

Fast Fact

The 1961-1963 model has the most nicknames of all T-Birds: Bullet Bird, Rocket Bird, Banana Bird, and Round Bird.

*Lee Iacocca, who later pushed for Ford's Mustang, helped hatch the 1962-1963 Thunderbird Sports Roadster. An optional **tonneau** cover made it look like a two seater.*

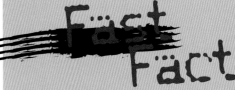

tonneau
    a shapely fiberglass panel that fits over the rear row of seating when the convertible top is down
horsepower
    a measure of mechanical power

Ford celebrated the 1,000,000 Thunderbird in 1972.

Sometimes Ford made radical changes to the Thunderbird design, such as making it a—yikes!—four door car in 1967. Even then, "suicide" (meet in the middle) doors declared that this T-Bird was no plain Jane jalopy.

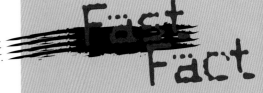

The six-barrel, big block M-code engine was a rare bird that could top 340 **horsepower** (hp). Collectors look for it mostly in Sports Roadsters.

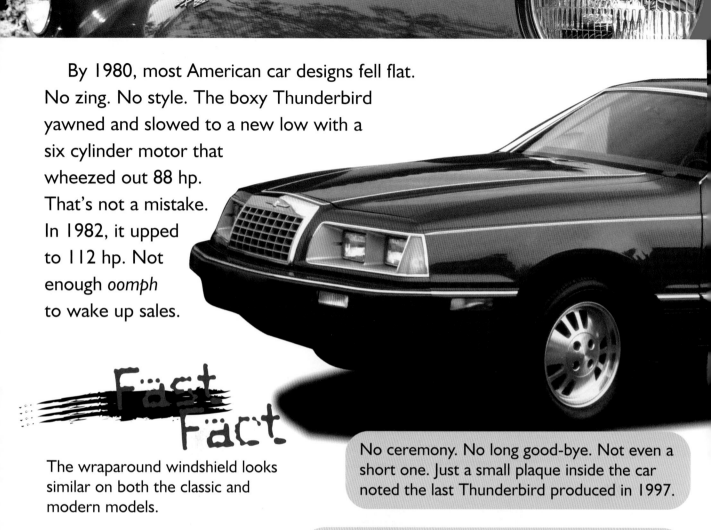

By 1980, most American car designs fell flat. No zing. No style. The boxy Thunderbird yawned and slowed to a new low with a six cylinder motor that wheezed out 88 hp. That's not a mistake. In 1982, it upped to 112 hp. Not enough *oomph* to wake up sales.

Fast Fact

The wraparound windshield looks similar on both the classic and modern models.

No ceremony. No long good-bye. Not even a short one. Just a small plaque inside the car noted the last Thunderbird produced in 1997.

Ford rounded the Thunderbird's disco stiff corners and trimmed its size for 1983. The new **aerodynamic** shape lowered wind drag and boosted performance. A **turbocharger** gave the Thunderbird engine a deep breath of air. The doldrums quickly blew away. By 1987, four cylinder Thunderbirds were kicking out 190 hp.

aerodynamic
: shaped so that air flows easily over the body at higher speeds

supercharger
: an engine with a device that adds air to help fuel burn more efficiently in the cylinders

turbocharger
: a special fan turned by the engine's exhaust gases that works to pump more air into the cylinders and boost power output

*Always tinkering, Ford totally updated the aerodynamic lines again and added a **supercharger** to a limited run of Thunderbirds in 1989. The extra air pumped serious thunder into these T-Birds. By 1994, the horsepower ratings hit 230. The low slung car could storm a quarter mile in just 15.8 seconds. Some hardcore fans have raced the Thunderbird SC.*

Today's Thunderbird SC racers have tuned the motors to nail a quarter mile in about 13 seconds.

15

Fifties Flashback

Ford caught America's retro trend at the end of the 1990s. The company made yet another radical Thunderbird design change with its new but classic concept car at the 1999 North American Auto Show in Detroit. Original style cues from the 1955 to 1957 models inspired the modern versions and reminded buyers of the T-Bird's youthful attitude.

Old Is New Again

- Just two seats
- Convertible roadster
- Removable hardtop with porthole windows
- Forward slash marks behind front wheels
- Round headlights and tail lights
- Oval grille with egg crate pattern
- Wraparound, slicked back windshield
- Hood scoop
- Two-tone interior
- Thunderbird badge

Through all of Ford's changes, Thunderbird kept some type of hood accent. The Retro 'Bird revived the flair of the original hood scoop. Special edition models used a chrome bezel on it.

aftermarket
> parts and accessories used to repair or enhance a product

Fast Fact

Customers could buy **aftermarket** chrome bezels for their painted hood scoops.

Fast Fact

Ford canceled the "fashion colors" Thunderbird Blue and Inspiration Yellow after 2002.

Ford designers turned to the 1955 color palette for ideas. They brought back Torch Red and Thunderbird Blue. For 2002 models, buyers could also choose Inspiration Yellow, Whisper White (not to be confused with Premium White offered later), or Evening Black.

Ford's design team revisited the long head-to-tail lines and forward stance of the 1960 and 1961 models. The new car adopted the early negative wedge stance. It made the front look slightly higher than the rear.

Fast Fact

The Retro Bird's top speed hovered around 140 mph (225 km/h).

Similar to the first Thunderbirds, the 2002 model tucked a brawny V-8 motor under the hood and used rear-wheel drive. Most modern cars use front-wheel drive— except sports cars. They have tended to use rear-wheel drive since the beginning.

Ford stirred interest among upscale shoppers with a Neiman Marcus Edition Thunderbird. Dressed in Evening Black with a Satin Silver metallic top, the car first wowed the crowds at the swanky 2000 Pebble Beach Concours d'Elegance.

Fast Fact

Neiman Marcus customers waited over a year to see their 2002 T-Birds.

Neiman Marcus 2000 Christmas Catalog hit mailboxes in September. It featured the limited-edition Neiman Marcus model for $41,995. All 200 cars sold out on the first day in just two hours and 15 minutes—the fastest ever for any car sold through this elite catalog. Ford dealers finally accepted orders for Retro Birds about four months later. Unfortunately, the factory didn't release the 2001 model year as planned. The new Thunderbird rolled out as a 2002 vehicle.

Fast Fact

The Neiman Marcus editions displayed the Thunderbird symbol in the porthole windows.

19

Ford announced it would cap production for the Retro Bird at 25,000 for 2002. Based on the company's monthly reports, it actually sold more than 30,000 cars. Sales dropped nearly in half after that and never perked up. The company started squawking about the end of the T-Bird. Ford officially canceled the car in July 2005. Again.

Each limited-edition "007" model has a unique plaque in the glove box with a serial number from 001 to 700.

The Award Winner Again

The 2002 Thunderbird earned many big awards just as the earlier models had done, including:

- The *Motor Week* Best Convertible for 2002
- eMotion! Reports.com Car of the Year
- The *Motor Trend* 2002 Car of the Year

Ford tried to build buyer interest in the $40,000 two-seater with a special-edition model in 2003. The "007" echoed the 2002 version driven by Halle Barry in the popular James Bond movie *Die Another Day*.

Fast Fact

The 2005 Thunderbirds carried a 50th Anniversary chevron on the fender.

The Fast Flyers

Winning racecars sell street cars. Even if the street Thunderbirds weren't fast flyers, Ford built a few early full-throttle Thunderbirds for the track. In 1957, Ford launched its Phase I Supercharged "Battlebirds." Two years later, the Thunderbird entered NASCAR racing and ran the first Daytona 500. It won six races that season.

Ford left NASCAR (the first time) in 1960. In 1978, a comeback with driver Bobby Allison grabbed a Ford victory at the Daytona 500.

In 1985, racecar driver Bill Elliot drove his Ford Thunderbird to victories at the Daytona 500, the Talladega Winston 500, and the Darlington Southern 500. He took home NASCAR's first $1-million bonus for winning three of the four "Big Four" superspeedway races. "Awesome Bill from Dawsonville" became "Million Dollar Bill" in his Thunderbird:

- **1985** Won 11 races
- **1985** Pictured on Sports Illustrated cover— first Cup driver ever
- **1986** Set a 212-mph qualifying speed record for the Talladega 500
- **1988** Won the Winston (now Nextel) Cup Championship
- **1992** Won four races in a row

The 1982 Thunderbird's aerodynamic design ruffled some feathers on the NASCAR circuit. The "Aero Bird" slipped through the wind and flew to first-place finishes at more than 150 top-division races, including four Daytona 500s.

NASCAR's "Intimidator," Dale Earnhardt, drove a Ford Thunderbird in 1982 and 1983.

Bill Elliot wasn't Ford's only big winner. Ford drivers claimed first place in 20 races in 1994. Rusty Wallace won eight of those races in his slick T-Bird. The next year, Mark Martin won four races.

The Thunderbird left NASCAR (again) in 1997, replaced by the Ford Taurus. Ford announced plans in 2006 to race the Fusion instead of the Taurus.

Ford won its first NASCAR manufacturer's title in 1992.

Fast Fact

Thunderbirds with modified engines have won major **drag racing** events around the world.

drag racing
    a test of automobile acceleration between two drivers

Star Cars

The Thunderbird filtered into America's music, movies, shopping, and other social experiences. Through its many designs, the T-Bird shined as the car of the stars and the star of cars.

Many Thunderbirds have cruised on the big screen. The 1973 career-launching movie *American Graffiti* tracked Suzanne Somers in a white T-Bird. Geena Davis and Susan Sarandon launched a 1966 convertible T-Bird in another critically acclaimed movie, 1991's *Thelma and Louise*.

A flash fire in 1967 aboard the *Apollo 1* spacecraft during a launch test killed three astronauts. Many companies then named products in honor of the lost NASA crew.

President John F. Kennedy used fifty 1961 Thunderbirds in his 1961 **inaugural** parade.

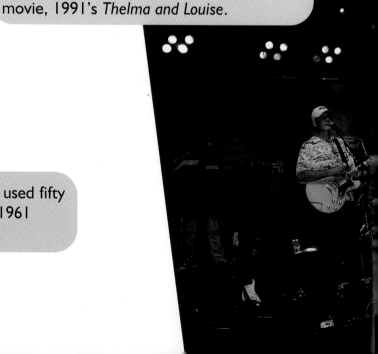

Abercrombie & Fitch (yes, that A & F) ordered five special "Apollo Thunderbirds" in 1967. Each of these fancy two-door birds wore metallic Apollo-blue paint and a matching blue vinyl top. Glitzy gadgets such as an electric sun roof, telephone, and television pumped up the price to $15,000 each. The show-cars lured shoppers to A & F stores in Miami, Palm Beach, New York, and Chicago. Sadly, San Francisco's car didn't survive the trek.

inaugural
the time of formal entry into office

Of all cars ever built, Thunderbird has won the most Motor Trend "Car of the Year" awards:
- **1958** Thunderbird
- **1965** Thunderbird and the entire Ford line
- **1987** Thunderbird Turbo Coupe
- **1989** Thunderbird Super Coupe
- **2002** Thunderbird

In 1971, Neiman Marcus offered "His and Her" Thunderbirds in its elite Christmas Catalog. These deluxe models featured telephones, tape recorders, and other special equipment. The pair cost only $25,000 (twice the price of ordinary cars).

Popular songs about the T-Bird have hit the airwaves for decades, from 1964's "Fun, Fun, Fun" by the Beach Boys to 1991's "Silver Thunderbird" by Marc Cohn. In the 1980s, a fun band tapped the powerful name, too: The Fabulous Thunderbirds.

Thunderbird fans around the world treasure the vehicles from each era. They gather at swap meets and street cruises. They share stories. They trade and sell parts. Because of the T-Bird's many major design differences, fan clubs tend to focus on specific years of cars instead of all Thunderbirds. These purists love to crow about their era's best features.

2005
1955 Ford Thunderbird

USA 37

The U.S. Postal service honored the 50th anniversary of the 1955 Ford Thunderbird with a commemorative stamp. Stamp collectors joined Thunderbird collectors and other car enthusiasts in an ongoing celebration of an American icon. The Thunderbird in its every design reflects America's trends over time. It's the nation's heritage on wheels.

Restoration takes countless hours of research, repairs, and refinishing. The Internet has helped to speed the process for many T-Bird fans.

The interest in vintage cars has boosted prices at auctions. The Barrett-Jackson Auction Company and other firms often sell beautiful Thunderbirds from every era for tens of thousands of dollars.

Glossary

acceleration (ak sehl ur AY shun) – an increase in speed

aerodynamic (ahr oh dih NAM ik) – air flows easily over the body for greater speed

aftermarket (AF tur mahr keht) – the market for parts and accessories used to repair or enhance a product

chassis (CHASS ee) – the frame that supports the body of a vehicle

drag racing (DRAG RAY seeng) – a test of pure automobile acceleration between two drivers

horsepower (HORS pow ur) – a measure of mechanical power; one horsepower equals 550 pounds (885 kg) lifted at one foot (30.5 cm) per second

inaugural (ihn AHG yer uhl) – the time of formal entry into office

restoration (reh stor AY shun) – to return something to its former condition

supercharger (SOO pur char jer) – an engine with a device that adds air to help fuel burn more efficiently in the cylinders

tonneau (TUHN o) – a shapely fiberglass panel that fits over the rear row of seating when the convertible top is down

turbocharger (TER bo char jer) – a special fan turned by the engine's exhaust gases that works to pump more air into the cylinders and boost power output

Further Reading

Elliot, Bill with Chris Millard. *Awesome Bill from Dawsonville: My Life in NASCAR*. HarperEntertainment, 2006.

Long, Brian. *The Book of the Ford Thunderbird from 1954*. Veloce, 2007.

Zuehlke, Jeffrey. *Classic Cars*. Lerner Publications, 2007.

Websites

www.intl-tbirdclub.com

www.tbird.org

Index

About the Author

Tracy Nelson Maurer writes nonfiction and fiction books for children, including more than 60 titles for Rourke Publishing LLC. Tracy lives with her husband Mike and two children near Minneapolis, Minnesota.